Ghost Stories
From the Texas
Hill Country

The Devil's Backbone

Bert Wall

EAKIN PRESS ★ AUSTIN, TEXAS

FIRST EDITION

Published in the United States of Ameica
by Eakin Press
A Division of Sunbelt Media, Inc.
P.O. Box 90159
Austin, TX 78709

2 3 4 5 6 7 8 9

ISBN 1-57168-104-3

Wall, Bert.
    Ghost stories from the Texas hill country's Devil's Backbone / by
Bert Wall.
        p.   cm.
    Includes bibliographical references and index.
    ISBN 1-57168-104-3 (alk. paper)
    1. Ghosts--Texas--Texas Hill Country.   2. Ghost stories--Texas-
-Texas Hill Country.   I. Title.
GR110.T5W35   1996
398.2'09764'05--dc20   96-24036
                                                                    CIP

To the memory of
N. R. "Pinky" Wall
and G. R. "Bob" Davis

Best wishes

Contents

Preface

Author Bert Wall has long considered himself a no-nonsense businessman who daily faced the reality of profit making. But growing up in both Houston and the Texas Hill Country, he became interested in the Devil's Backbone, a ridge of mountains that stretch along the Blanco River between the tourist village of Wimberley and the old Texas community of Blanco. Growing up, Bert was aware of the stories of the supernatural that old timers would tell. He began collecting the tales and in 1996 segments of four of those stories were on the nationally acclaimed television series *Unsolved Mysteries* on the ABC network. Success in real estate allowed Bert his dream, to own a ranch on the Devil's Backbone, where he and his wife make their home today. Twenty-two stories, including Drago's Indian, are featured in this first volume. A fifth-generation Texan, Bert attended the University of Houston, where he majored in history and political science.

Acknowledgements

To all those who assisted in the writing of this book I am deeply indebted.

Therer are many friends and associates who experiences are recounted here which help make this work a reality.

I will be forever grateful to William Greene, Clifford Davis, and Mary Davis, whose support has been invaluable.

Finally, a special thanks to my wife Carolyn "C. D." Wall, who took on the task of editing and typing this manuscript.

The Devil's Backbone

The mysteriously unique region known as the Devil's Backbone is located in the Central Texas Hill Country between the small cities of San Marcos and Blanco, and is a few minutes drive from either the recreational Canyon Lake or the quaint community of Wimberley. It is only a one-hour drive from either San Antonio or Austin, so should you be traveling in the vicinity you may want to venture onto Highway 32 which meanders its way across the four mile stretch of this majestic countryside. The highway markers posted at each end of the Backbone will designate your crossing, and you might want to pull into the roadside park to fully enjoy the spectacular views.

The Backbone's rugged hills, near 1400 feet in elevation, drop off into deep canyons and lush green valleys which are encompassed by crystal-clear, spring-fed creeks and streams. While its rocky terrain is predominately blanketed with juniper and oak trees, you can still find an occasional cottonwood, black walnut, dogwood, or the endangered madrone. The plantlife on the Backbone ranges from a variety of wildflowers and cactus that display their colorful red, pink, and yellow blooms each spring, to a few wild grapevines that have

1

entwined themselves in the underbrush that lines the creekbanks. Since a wide variety of wildlife still inhabits this unspoiled country, you may be just as apt to see a graceful whitetail deer as you are a deadly diamondback rattlesnake.

The history of the Devil's Backbone is just as intriguing as its beauty. Very few records show much in the way of expedition into the small region until 1757. It was then that General Miranda crossed the area while on a mission for the Spanish monarchy. Since Miranda had been quite successful in his search for gold in Peru, he had gained recognition from the Spanish throne, and was subsequently assigned to begin a search for the Seven Cities of Gold. This search led Miranda and his men across the Devil's Backbone.

One theory as to how this region acquired its name is that, as was customary, a member of the Catholic Church accompanied the expedition and had almost as much authority as the officer in charge. It is said that the monk, named Espinoza, was so extremely cruel and mean in his demands of the laborers that they had nicknamed him Diablo. Then, when they began forging their way across this particularly rugged pass they called it Espinoza Diablo, which when translated into the English language means Devil's Backbone.

At first the Spaniards were welcomed by the Lipan Apache and Comanche Indians, who were the main tribes inhabiting this wilderness. Then the Spaniards began enslaving the Indians, so they went on the warpath and drove the intruders out of the area.

Around 1845 the strong-willed, but fair-minded, German immigrants started moving into Central Texas searching for a new land and beginning. They soon befriended the Indians and became one of the very few groups of people in the U.S. to enter into a treaty with them.

By the late 1870s the treaty came to an end, only because the U.S. had forced the Indians off of their native lands and onto reservations. For all practical purposes, the Indian had disappeared from this region, but their sacred burial grounds still remain.

The Backbone was no stranger to the outlaws that the Civil War produced. It had been reported that such men as Jesse and Frank James sought refuge with the local ranchers on more than one occasion.

All types of individuals have crossed the Devil's Backbone on their journeys West, and even today, in some remote areas, you may stumble onto artifacts that evidence their passing. You may find an old wagon wheel from the days of the Spanish expeditions, an arrowhead that once belonged to a proud Indian, a spent casing from the gun of a cowboy or outlaw, or perhaps you might run across a mine shaft that was abandoned by an old prospector. Then there are the unusal standing rocks that are sprinkled across these hills — perhaps they are the unmarked tombstones of those travelers who ended their journey here on the Devil's Backbone.

There are believers and non-believers as to the existence of spirtual beings from the past. This is each individual's decision, but as you read on, you may find yourself reconsidering that option.

If you ever happen to stop at the roadside park atop the Devil's Backbone, don't be surprised at what you might see.

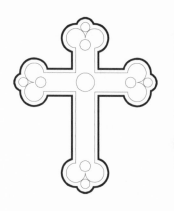

The Spanish Monk

For the benefit of those who might not be familiar with the history of our Central Texas area, I would just like to mention that the 1700s were quite active with Spanish expeditions crossing through this part of the country. This is documented in several records, including the famous *Miranda Report*, which was written for the King of Spain in 1757. As was customary, a member of the Catholic Church was always assigned to accompany these expeditions. So much for that bit of history. Now we shall move on with the following story which took place in early December 1987.

Our ranch house sits atop a high hill along the old Devil's Backbone in Central Texas. When the north wind blows on a cold winter's night, such as it did this particular evening, the house creaks and moans with sounds that seem to wake the old spirits from the past.

It was approaching midnight, and I was attempting to finish up writing a novel which we had been working on for at least two years. By then I was on my fourth pot of coffee, and Lord knows how many cigarettes, and I had become mentally exhausted. Since

4

my eyes could also use a rest, I decided to take a short break.

After throwing another log into the fireplace and pouring another cup of coffee, I sat down in my easy chair and began staring out the window which overlooks a deck outside. I took off my glasses to rub my tired eyes, and as I continued sipping the steaming cup of coffee, I became aware of how dark this particular night really was. There was absolutely no moon in God's heaven, and with the overcast sky, it was pitch-black outside. When I finished my coffee, and was just about to get back to writing, I heard one of our dogs start barking. I could tell that this older dog was either on or near the front deck, and that her bark was of a friendly nature, not one of fright or danger. Within seconds she was again quiet, as if she had only barked to announce the arrival of someone she knew. I didn't hear a car pull up to the house, and I couldn't think of anyone we knew who would be out that late on such a cold winter's night, so I didn't check outside.

I went back to writing and, within a minute or two, I had an eerie feeling that someone was staring in at me. It was then I looked up and first saw him — standing at the window was what appeared to be a Spanish monk, who on this pitch-dark night, was illuminated in a soft-pink glow.

I figured I was just over-exhausted, and that my eyes were playing a trick on me, so I shut my eyes and tried shaking my head to clear the cobwebs from my mind. When I looked again, he was still there, and this time I was able to see the large crucifix hanging from his waist. I couldn't see his face because the hood of his gray-brown robe was pulled up over his head. The robe appeared to be made of a heavy burlap or woolen material, which I believe must have come from the 1700s era.

Even though it seemed like an eternity, I know it must have been just a matter of seconds before he started moving away from the window, as if he was going to walk on down the deck. I jumped to my feet and ran to the door, hoping to get a closer look at this spirit from the past. By the time I stepped outside, he had vanished.

For some unknown reason, I was privileged to see that Spanish monk, who traveled this land centuries ago. I have often wondered if he could have been Espinoza, the monk from whom, as one theory has it, the Devil's Backbone acquired its name.

Children's
Voices

The summers are quite hot on the old Devil's Backbone, and that particular mid-August afternoon of 1992 was certainly no exception. The relentless sun was beating down on the rough, rocky hills, and it had to have been at least 110 degrees in the shade.

Jesse and Harry had been working on fence repairs since early morning, and had just finished stretching the last roll of barbed wire across the old cedar fence posts. They had started the repairs on top of a high hill and ended up in a sparse, wooded valley. It was there, deep within the hidden valley, that they decided it was surely time to take a much deserved break. Jesse knew this valley well, for he had worked on the ranch many times over the last few years, but it was only the second time Harry had been down there.

With Jesse in the lead, they made a bee-line to the cold water of the narrow, spring-fed creek. These cowboys were wringing wet with sweat which, now mixed with dust, had created a thin coating of yellow mud that clung to their clothing. Even their black cowboy hats had changed color during the day. Jesse quickly pulled off his boots, haphazardly tossed his hat aside, and then jumped into the crystal-clear water, clothes and all. Harry soon followed suit.

After several minutes of swimming and washing the mud from their clothes, they crawled out of the creek and found some shade to rest under. Sitting with their backs propped up against the trees, Jesse then began a rather one-sided conversation. "Man, its been a hot one today. Good thing we quit when we did. Don't think I coulda made it too much longer. How 'bout you?" Harry just nodded in full agreement, and Jesse continued, "Not tryin' to change the subject, but this valley is one weird place . . ."

Harry wasn't really listening because he had become preoccupied with taking in the full beauty of the mysteriously captivating hidden valley. On his previous trip down there he had been in and out so briefly that he didn't have a chance to really look around. He now realized that the rugged, high hills completely surrounded the valley, and that the creekbed ran all the way around the base of the hills.

It was about then that Harry suddenly began to smell gardenias, but there were certainly no gardenias around; only some oak and a few cedar trees lined the bank of the creek. The scent became much stronger and it seemed to surround him, but then it faded away. He interrupted Jesse, who had only paused to catch his breath. "Did you smell that? Smelled like the old-timey gardenia perfume my grandma used to call toilet water."

Jesse answered with a half-knowing smirk on his face. "Yep, I smelled it, but there sure ain't no gardenia bushes around here. Like I've been tryin' to tell ya, I've seen and heard some mighty strange things down here. There's quite a few old-timers' tales about this place. A lot of folks believe this valley is haunted."

Harry, again only half-listening, pulled his boots back on, and was still trying to figure out where the gardenia smell had come from. Jesse was making only a feeble attempt at pulling his boots back on, since he was thoroughly enjoying their break and was in no hurry to get back to work.

Then Harry briefly heard the voices of young children. It seemed to him that they were laughing and splashing around in the upper creek, not too far away. He gave Jesse a questioning look, "Wonder where they came from? There ain't no kids livin' anywhere near this ranch. I'm gonna go run'um off. They could get hurt way down here." Jesse didn't have time to answer before long-legged Harry started sprinting up the creek.

Within seconds Harry reached the spot where he thought he had heard the children's voices, but no one was there. He thought to himself, they couldn't have gotten away that quickly. Then he saw that the water was still rippling where they must have just crawled out of the creek, so he yelled out, only half expecting the children to come out of hiding. Harry wasn't surprised that he didn't get an answer, until he looked around and then realized that there was virtually no place that the children could be hiding — it was as if they had vanished.

Harry just stood there for awhile, trying to figure it all out, and then finally gave up. As he turned to head back down the creek, he caught a glimpse of something lying on the ground. He kneeled down, and picked up a small, tattered pouch, which was about the size of his hand. He felt that the pouch must have been white at one time, and had just turned a brownish-yellow color due to age. As he gingerly turned it over for further examination, he saw a faded inscription that gave him one heck of a chill. It read "Rock Candy — Atlanta, Georgia — 1843." This was just the kind of candy bag a child would have carried — but it would have been many, many years ago.

Harry was quickly becoming convinced that there just might be something to the old-timers' tales, and that the valley just might be haunted. Maybe the voices were those of children from the past — maybe the scent of gardenias was their mother's perfume.

If you were to talk to Harry today, he probably wouldn't say a word about that strange valley — but I'll bet if he ever has to go back down there, he won't go alone.

It was before the days of daylight savings time, and more particularly in the early 1950s, when as a very small boy I witnessed the strange lady in white.

Oh, in some ways I wish those days would return, life was much simpler then, and the smallest pleasure was a true experience. We were raised just outside of Wimberley on the Blanco River. At that time Wimberley was a town of approximately 750 people — cowboys, cedar choppers, ranchers, and true western characters made up our population.

Saturdays were big days for my brother and I, for Saturday was the day that we would make our weekly trek to San Marcos so our mother could take care of all the in-town chores. First we would go to the grocery store, then the feed store, and then the old San Marcos Telephone Company where she would make the necessary phone calls that had piled up during the previous week (in the early Fifties we still did not have our own telephone service in the Wimberley area). After the calls were made and all of the shopping chores were taken care of, if we had been well-behaved, my brother and I were treated to a movie at the old Texas

11

Theater. It was after one of those Saturdays that the following event took place.

It must have been about 8:30 P.M. when Mom pulled the old 1949 Ford out of the theater parking lot in San Marcos and headed out Ranch Road 12 towards Wimberley. It was pitch black (or as the old timers would say "it was good dark") and there was not another car on the road as we made our way towards Wimberley. Perched on a large box which was sitting on the back seat I was able to balance myself and watch the road just as if I were driving the old Ford.

We were at least six or seven miles out of San Marcos when the lady appeared. She was dressed in a brilliantly white evening gown which looked to have been from the 1800s. The lady quickly crossed the road, moving from left to right. My mother's reflexes were good and as she swerved to miss the lady she steered the car to the right hitting the road's shoulder. By the time the car had come to a complete stop we were just inches from that majestic oak tree which stands in the highway's right-of-way.

It had all happened so fast that my mother just sat there for a minute or two. She then quickly checked us boys to be sure we were all right and then, without saying a word, she grabbed a flashlight and got out of the car. As best as I can remember she walked across the highway and yelled out several times. She could find no one — the lady in white had disappeared.

As local legend goes, the lady in white had been seen before that incident, and has been seen many times since. In fact there have been several automobile accidents in that same area over the years — so if you ever venture out on Ranch Road 12 after dark be on the lookout for the lady in white.

The Predator

It was an extremely hot August afternoon in 1983 and we were finishing up the last mile of fencing on one of the Devil's Backbone ranches. It had been one rough project, and were glad to see the job coming to an end.

One of the older gentlemen in the group is quite a story in his own right. Now in his early eighties, he saw action in WWII and was decorated for his tour of duty in the Pacific theater. This story has nothing to do with his heroics, however, it does concern the many years he has worked along these canyons and hills of Central Texas.

I was observing the gentleman that hot afternoon as he gazed across one of those deep canyons along the Backbone, and when he took his hat off to wipe the sweat from his brow he began to chuckle. I gently patted him on his back and asked him what was so funny. He replied, "Oh, not much son. I just couldn't help remembering something that happened right here several decades ago. Guess I've been around this old country too long." After a little coaxing he told me the following story.

It was 1948 (the war had just ended a few years

13

before) and most things in Central Texas were getting back to normal, with one exception. It seems there was a predator on the loose that had the local ranchers up in arms. The animal killer stalked an area from the Ranch Road 12 and Highway 32 junction westward, on past the Devil's Backbone towards Blanco. It's prey of cattle, sheep, and goats were spread across the countryside.

First, the ranchers set baited traps in hopes of catching the predator, but they had no luck with that technique. Next they, along with their hunting dogs, combed the hills in an attempt to track down the animal, but no one even caught a glimpse of the elusive killer. After trying everything they knew, the ranchers gathered together and decided it was then time to hire a professional hunter. Back in those days a professional hunter was considered to be dang near as much a predator as the ones he stalked.

The word went out, and within a short time such a character (an older man who had spent most of his time in the Guadalupe Mountains of West Texas) met with the ranchers at the old Forrester's Drug Store (now the Cypress Creek Cafe) in the small town of Wimberley. He told the ranchers he wanted no contact with them after he set up his camp, which would be in a small valley just below one of the Backbone's ridges. Then he reassured them that within 30 days he would be back with their predator, collect his pay, and head back west.

Some thirty-five days later the hunter reappeared at Forrester's. He was obviously tired and haggard and quite anxious to leave. He relayed the following report to the ranchers.

Not long after setting up camp he found the predator's trail, and then he wasted no time setting his traps. He had no luck with that technique. He would find the traps sprung, but the bait untouched. This gave him the impression that the predator was playing some sort of game with him, and he sensed that *he* had become the prey being stalked both day and night.

After many days of no results in tracking the elusive predator or finding it's resting place, he finally got lucky.

It was late one afternoon as he sat on a high ridge, and when he saw the "predator" he couldn't believe his eyes. It was a goat. Yes, an enormous white ram weighing at least 200 pounds. This beast had huge red eyes and appeared to exhale fire from its nostrils.

Finally, the hunter had found the predator's resting place, and within minutes he reached the entrance to a cave. As he peered inside and saw the glow of the beast's red eyes intently staring back at him a cold chill ran up his spine. He then realized that this animal was truly not afraid of anything.

He raised his rifle, aimed between the goat's eyes and fired. Then a sound roared in his ears, but it was not that of rifle fire. This particular sound, he knew only too well, was that of rattlesnakes.

He jumped back to catch his breath and took a small flashlight from a pouch that hung around his neck. Then he slowly moved back to the entrance to review the situation.

Now, with the aid of some light, he saw the goat was lying down and saw a small pool of blood under it's chin. The beast's red eyes were still open and fixed on the cave's entrance. The rattlesnakes, literally hundreds of them, were everywhere. Towards the back of the cave he caught a glimpse of several chests and what appeared to be some gold coins lying on the floor.

Upon finishing this report the hunter wasted no time in collecting his pay, and as he opened the cafe door to leave, he turned to the ranchers and said, "The Devil. Yep, I was hunting the Devil . . . and he's still out there."

After his departure the massive predatory slaughter of livestock did cease for several decades — but what about the slayings out on the Backbone just three short years ago?

Mystery Riders

This tale begins late one night shortly after the Civil War had come to an end, while a group of men from a local community were returning home from a hunting trip in the hills that lay west of San Marcos. One of the men was climbing a canyon wall, and when he began to lose his footing, he grabbed a ledge to catch his fall. A piece of rock from the ledge broke off in his hand, and for some unknown reason he decided to put it in his pocket. Days later, he had the rock assayed, to learn that it contained a high-grade silver ore. As the legend goes, until their deaths, these men continually searched for, but were never able to relocate that particular canyon which they believed might contain a ledge of silver ore.

It had been a cold, wet December day in 1986, but that night a full moon had poked its way through the clouds. Joel, the Chaparral's ranch foreman, had eaten dinner early and decided to read for awhile before turning in. As some of us tend to do, he had become so engrossed in reading that he had lost all conception of time, until he was distracted by the sound of horses galloping past his quarters.

It was around midnight when Joel stepped outside to see if the corral gate had been accidently left open. When he saw the gate was closed, he went ahead and checked the stall area anyway. All of our horses were accounted for, just as they had been earlier when he fed and locked them in for the night.

Joel didn't give the incident too much more thought and then went on to bed. At approximately 3:00 A.M. he was again awakened by the rumble of galloping horses. When he looked out the window he was shocked to see five or six horsemen who had slowed their steeds to a trot as they neared his quarters. He quickly pulled on his boots, grabbed his coat and bolted out the door. Joel was fully expecting an encounter of some sort — but the riders had disappeared into the night. Needless to say, he was quite leery about this situation, but there was nothing more he could do about it at that hour of the morning.

At daybreak he checked the muddy ground for hoof prints, which would at least give him some indication of which direction the horsemen had taken — no tracks could be found.

When Joel told me what had happened, he described the riders as best he could. He said that, in the moonlight, it looked like the men were wearing old-styled western dusters and weather-beaten hats, resembling those worn by the Confederate Cavalry.

This description triggered my memory of other tales I had heard about some mysterious horsemen being spotted in the area from time to time. In 1932 there were several sightings as Highway 32 was being routed across the Devil's Backbone. Then, in 1945, there was the well-respected, long-time resident cowboy who suddenly packed up his family and moved out of the area. It is rumored that late one night, after tending to his cattle, he was crossing the Backbone when he was confronted by the horsemen.

No one seems to know who the mystery riders are — perhaps those hunters from many years ago are still searching for their lost ledge of silver.

Supernatural Sunday

It was an unseasonably mild and warm Super Bowl Sunday in 1989 on the old Devil's Backbone. Our son, B. C., along with several of his friends, arrived early in the afternoon to take full advantage of the beautiful weather. These young college men really enjoyed coming out to the ranch, sometimes just to relax around the house, but more often to venture out and explore the undisturbed high hills, deep canyons, and dry creekbeds.

I was outside tending to the barbeque pits when the group arrived. After we visited for a short while, some of the group went into the house for snacks, and some gathered at the barn area for a game of basketball.

With this lively group's comings and goings between the house and the barn, and all the pre-game activities taking place, a couple of hours slipped by before I noticed B. C., John, and Corey weren't around. When I glanced down towards the barn and saw that the ranch truck was gone, I figured they must have taken off to do some exploring.

When the trio returned they didn't stop at the barn, but instead drove up to the house to park the truck. I casually noticed that when John and Corey got out that they went straight into the house. When B. C. walked over to join me at the barbeque pits it was quite apparent that his previously jovial mood had become one of deep concern. He had a worried, disbelieving look on his face, as if he were off in another world. He didn't say a thing, and all he seemed able to do was walk around and shake his head. Having witnessed this reaction of disbelief from many others who have visited the Chaparral, I immediately suspected that a supernatural encounter of some sort had taken place. When B. C. finally spoke, only to say that something weird had happened to John, I knew my suspicions would be confirmed. I asked him what had happened, but all he could say was that I needed to hear it from John. Since I knew a first-hand accounting would be the most accurate, and I was quite anxious to hear what had happened, I asked him to go see if John and Corey would come outside while I finished the barbeque duty.

Within a couple of minutes the trio took their seats on some boulders that are randomly placed under the large oak trees of the barbeque area, but no one said a word. I have learned over the many years of gathering these spiritual accountings that it is best not to start immediately questioning the individual as to what took place. Wait, let them take their time, and when they are ready to speak, their story will flow out as steadily as water from an open faucet.

John sat quietly for quite some time, and I could tell from the expression on the face of this good-looking young man of Mexican and Apache heritage that he must have gone through one heck of an experience. His accounting will follow, but first I will give you a brief description of what we refer to as Haunted Valley, which is where the three young men had gone to explore that day.

Haunted Valley is approximately twenty-five

acres of flat land with high grass in which an old rock tank, a windmill, and a dilapidated pole-barn are located. This valley is surrounded by steep mountains of extremely rough, rocky terrain, thickly covered with cedar and oak trees, cactus, century plants and several other types of vegetation. At the base of the mountains, also surrounding the valley, is a rock-bottom creekbed. It's embankments are densely covered with underbrush, and in some places the tops of huge oak trees have grown completely across the creekbed resulting in dark tunnel areas.

Now for John's accounting of what took place after the truck was parked at the edge of the valley and all three young men began exploring the creekbed together. It wasn't long before John found himself alone, but since it isn't uncommon for explorers to take off in different directions, he didn't give it a second thought.

As he continued walking up the creekbed, just before entering one of the tunnel areas, he knelt down to take a closer look at a crystal rock that had been glistening in the sun. Suddenly an extremely cold chill came upon him, as if he had stepped into a walk-in freezer. When he attempted to stand up he found that gravity was playing a trick on him or some other force had paralyzed him in the kneeling position. Within a split-second John heard something rustling along the embankment. Then he saw it — a large silver-gray wolf — surrounded by a strange haze of some sort. The animal was crouched in a small clearing directly above him.

John was petrified since he was still unable to stand up. All he could do was hope this predator would move on.

Suddenly, without provocation, the wolf leaped.

It passed through John's body — I repeat — it passed *through* his body . . . there was no impact at all . . . the wolf was gone.

At the moment the wolf seemingly exited John's body he fell backwards, as if finally released from the force that had magnetized him in the kneeling position.

John scrambled to his feet and yelled out for B. C. and Corey. He ran back to the truck where he found them waiting for him. He told them what had happened and that for some reason he was still really cold. They got into the truck and started back to the house. By the time they reached the top of the mountain John's chill was gone but he felt something was still inside him.

As John finished his accounting, I was convinced that he had entered a cold zone — a spirited area. I strongly suspected that somehow, by way of the wolf, John was given a gift that only a very few people seem to develop — a gift of insight into the spiritual world.

With the rest of the guys completely unaware of John's experience, the Super Bowl party continued. Soon after the game was over, all of the young men returned to San Marcos. But there is more concerning John's encounter in "Late Night Caller."

Late Night Caller

By nightfall the unseasonably mild and warm weather we had enjoyed the afternoon of Super Bowl Sunday 1989 had given way to a typical January storm. The temperature dropped considerably when the thirty-five mph northerly wind began to blow across the hills of the Devil's Backbone. By mid-evening the sheets of rain and sleet began their descent on the Chaparral Ranch. There was no doubt we were in for a cold, rough night, but I still remember the strange feeling that came over me as I lit the logs in the fireplace — the feeling that something completely unexpected would happen before the break of day.

My son B. C. and a group of his college friends had gathered at our home earlier that day to enjoy some festivities and watch the Super Bowl with me, my wife C. D., and our long-time friend Robert, who was living with us at the time.

The television had been turned off after the game ended, and with the young men headed back to San Marcos, the three of us were enjoying the peace and quiet that followed the somewhat hectic afternoon. C. D. was busy cleaning the kitchen, Robert had settled down with a book, and I started cleaning our hunting rifles.

Around 10:00 P.M. C. D. finished the kitchen chores and went straight to bed, and a short while later Robert retired to his bedroom. I stayed up another hour or so finishing the chore I had started, still trying to figure out why I couldn't shake that strange premonition. I remember thinking that maybe I was just feeling uneasy because of John's experience earlier that afternoon.

With my chore completed, I put on my sleeping gown, climbed into bed and turned off the lights. I laid there quite awhile just listening to the crackling of the fire in the fireplace, and through our bedroom doorway, I watched the shadows the flames had cast across the living room walls. I remember thinking how closely those majestic shadows resembled Indians dancing a silent ritual.

Around midnight I finally began to dose off, but became fully alert when I heard "Dad . . . Dad" being called out.

When I flipped on the bedside lamp I saw B. C. standing in the bedroom doorway. Even though his face was flushed and he was noticeably unnerved, he calmly told me that John had gone "a little crazy," and had insisted on coming back out to the ranch. So as not to disturb C. D.'s sleep, I got out of bed and followed B. C. into the living room and shut the bedroom door behind me.

To my surprise, the only one in the living room was Robert, who had been awakened when he heard the car pull up in the driveway. B. C. headed back outside, saying he needed to go help Corey with John. Apparently, as soon as the car was parked, John lept out. On this cold, bleak winter night he took off on foot across this rough, rugged country.

I was putting another log on the fire when the trio

came in the back door, B. C. and Corey guiding John through the kitchen into the living room. They literally had to place John in a chair next to the fireplace, then they joined Robert, who was sitting on the sofa. I took a seat directly across from John so I could fully observe this young man. He just sat there in complete silence, seemingly unaware of anyone's presence.

B. C. and Corey quickly filled me in on what had happened after they got back to San Marcos. Before returning to their dormitory, they stopped at a local pizza parlor for some coffee, and while they were there John became completely preoccupied in thought. John, who is a fun-loving, jovial, somewhat talkative young man, was unusually quiet and didn't respond to any conversation around him. From time to time other friends would stop by their table to rehash the Super Bowl game, but John just sat there quietly staring out the window.

Around 11:00 P.M. they decided to head towards the dorm, but as they were getting in the car John muttered that he had to go back out to the ranch — right then. At first B. C. and Corey thought he was just joking around, but by the time they reached the dorm parking lot they knew John was quite serious. He couldn't give them a reason why he wanted to go to the ranch, but he had become insistant, almost to the point of violence. He was going, with or without them. Since John isn't the insistant, much less violent type, it was obvious to B. C. and Corey that something was definitely wrong. So the three of them headed back towards the Chaparral.

During most of the drive from San Marcos to the ranch John sat silently in a preoccupied state of mind. When he finally did speak, it was not John's voice that B .C. and Corey heard. They had never heard that voice, and they didn't understand what he was saying because he was chanting in some sort of foreign language.

By the time they parked the car in our driveway, B.C. and Corey were quite frightened. John had jumped out of the car, and they had to restrain him from wandering off across the dark countryside. Within seconds John slipped back into silence and calmed down enough for them to lead him into the house.

John sat silently staring at the fire as B. C. and Corey concluded relating the above events to Robert and I. Then B. C. suggested that if I talked to John, with no one else around, he might straighten up and tell me what was wrong. It was worth a try, so B. C., Corey, and Robert went into the kitchen,where they could still observe what was taking place in the living room.

Now for the somewhat difficult task of describing to you what took place after I simply asked John what was bothering him. He didn't say a word — but immediately seemed to lose control of his body. His arms and legs twisted in all sorts of directions, as if he were double-jointed. His breathing was frightfully irregular, his chest and stomach twisting in and out of shape with every breath he took. Somehow, he managed to stabilize his head against the back of the chair, but it was tilted in such a way that only the whites of his eyes were visible. Every now and then I could tell that he attempted to regain control of his body, but within seconds he would slip back into those wild contortions.

The rest of us didn't know what to do, and it seemed like an eternity before John calmed down. His arms and legs still jerked sporadically, and his breathing was still somewhat irregular, but his chest and stomach were not affected. He was able to hold his head upright, and once again his eyes became fixed on the dancing flames in the fireplace. Finally, he seemed to regain complete control of his body.

Suddenly, John began to speak — but the voice I heard was not John's. Later, B. C. and Corey told me it was the same voice they had heard earlier in the car — but this time the language being spoken was English.

In this deeper, much older man's voice, John began describing a bloody battle between two Indian tribes. It was as if he had a ring-side seat, giving me a blow-by-blow description of the battle.

I have no doubt that for some unknown reason an Indian's spirit had chosen John as a medium to relay the events of that particular battle to me. The pain he must have felt was now quite visible on John's face as he described every gruesome detail.

From what I was able to gather, the battle took place back in the early 1800s, after this spirit's tribe and a rival tribe had both claimed sacred ground rights to a certain piece of land. Now, as I consider the vivid description John recounted, I have no doubt that the sacred land they fought for is within the boundaries of the Chaparral.

This spirit was present for some five to ten minutes, then, within a split-second, he aburptly concluded his communication.

A strong gust of wind blew across the living room, then whistled into the kitchen where B. C., Corey, and Robert were standing in awe of what had taken place. As the wind dissipated through the closed kitchen window, and its whistle faded into the cold, bleak darkness outside, we knew our late night caller was gone.

John closed his eyes and dosed off for only a brief moment while the rest of us just stared at each other in utter disbelief.

When John awoke, he sat straight up in his chair, and quite obviously confused, asked what he was doing back at the ranch — he had no recollection of what had happened.

A couple of hours passed as we all sat discussing the night's events, and finally B. C., Corey, and John had to leave.

John has been out to the Chaparral many times since that night — but as far as I know, our late night caller has never returned.

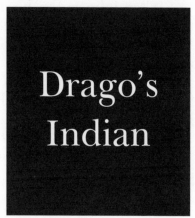

Drago's Indian

It took Bart Johns two or three years before he told me about the following encounter which took place on the Devil's Backbone in November of 1981.

Bart was deer hunting that day, and just before dusk he started walking out of the woods towards the truck which was parked a short distance away. Almost as soon as he stepped out of the deer stand, the feeling of being stalked came over him, and by the time he reached the road he was positive he was being watched.

He had gone no more than ten to twenty feet down the road when he turned to look behind him. He was shocked to see an Indian — yes, an *Indian*. Bart called out for the man to identify himself, but the Indian silently stood in place with his crossed arms, cradling an old-style buffalo gun.

Bart spoke again, and then the Indian started walking towards him — but there was absolutely no noise of any kind. It was as if Bart had temporarily gone deaf.

At that point, Bart became completely unnerved, and all he wanted to do was to get out of there. He started running towards the truck, but he felt like he was running in slow motion, and he couldn't see the truck which he knew was just a few feet ahead . . . it was as if the truck had disappeared.

When he glanced back over his shoulder, he saw that the Indian was still following him, but was veering to the side of the road. Then, all of a sudden, the Indian seemed to simply vanish into the woods — and Bart ran full-force smack into the truck. He could then hear some of the other hunters yelling to each other as they were tracking a deer that had been shot just at dusk — during Bart's encounter with the Indian he hadn't even heard the shots that had been fired.

When Bart related this incident to me he said he was positive he had been controlled by some sort of force, and he felt like he had been trapped in some other era of time — perhaps he was.

The Indian Bart described was dressed in old-western clothing and wore a tall crowned, flat-brimmed, black hat — the style of hat that was quite popular with the Indians back in the late 1800s.

A few months after Bart told us about his experience, my wife was shopping at a local antique shop, and couldn't resist buying an old oil painting by an artist named Drago.

The painting, which still hangs in our living room, is of an Indian — dressed in old-western clothing, wearing a tall crowned, flat-brimmed, black hat — thus we call this tale "Drago's Indian."

Haunted Valley

Haunted Valley lies tucked away within the folds of the Devil's Backbone. It is approximately 25 acres of flat land blanketed in lush blue-stem grass. It is completely engulfed by steep mountains of extremely rough, rocky terrain, which is hidden beneath thick growths of cedar and oak trees, cactus, and century plants. At the base of the mountains, also emcompassing the valley, is a rock-bottom creekbed with its embankments densely overgrown by several other types of vegetation.

There are no paved roads leading to Haunted Valley, and driving to it does require the use of a 4-wheel drive vehicle. The main road to the valley meanders and snakes down a mountain, and towards the bottom there is an overhang of trees that form a type of tunnel which ends at the western edge of the valley.

An old rock tank, a windmill, a hand-carved timber loading ramp, and a dilapidated pole-barn are located at the valley's eastern edge.

My wife and I always enjoy the tranquility that this valley offers us, but there are others who simply cannot.

My brother is now in his mid-forties, and both he and I are experienced hunters and outdoorsmen. Neither he nor I have ever feared nature's surroundings, so the following incident was completely unexpected.

One afternoon, a few months before deer season of 1980, we were checking several areas on the ranch for deer tracks, and eventually ended up in Haunted Valley. We hadn't been down there too long before I sensed that something was bothering my brother. He suddenly announced that he wanted to leave, so I asked him what was wrong. He barely had time to say that he really felt uncomfortable before a rather strong breeze blew through the valley. The breeze wasn't cool enough to have raised a chill. He turned to me, and with a strange look on his face, remarked that he was cold. At that point he became very insistent on leaving.

We returned to the truck, started out of the valley, and as we approached the top of the mountain, he made the following comments that I will never forget — "Bert, I don't know if there are such things as ghosts, but if there are, that valley down there has *got* to be haunted. For some crazy reason I just have a gruesome feeling that something terrible, like a murder or massacre, took place down there."

From that day to present, we refer to that valley as Haunted Valley, and even now, years later, my brother will not stay down in that valley for more than an hour at any one time.

During the summer of 1986 the following story was related to me by Sam Wilson, a local craftsman we have known for quite some time.

Sam doesn't hunt just for the pure sport of deer hunting. Occasionally, only when absolutely necessary, he will go deer hunting to provide meat for his family. He use to saddle-up his old, gray-black mare and ride down to Haunted Valley where he would almost always be assured of finding some game.

It was a cold, gray day in early January many years ago, and by the time Sam reached the valley, which is some ten miles from his home, it was near dark. There was no time to waste. He quickly dismounted his mare and tied her reins to a small oak tree near the edge of the valley. Then he took cover in the thick cedar breaks.

Within a couple of minutes, a strange feeling began to come over him, but he shrugged it off when he spotted a large doe entering the valley.

Since Sam is an excellent rifleman he had to fire only one shot, and the doe fell dead in her tracks.

As he crossed the valley that strange feeling, an uneasy feeling of being watched by someone, resurfaced, but Sam knew the chances of someone else being anywhere near that valley were slim to none. When he scanned the countryside he felt assured that no other human was in the area. He quickly field-dressed the deer, draped her carcass across his broad shoulders, and started back towards his horse.

The dark of night closed in before he reached the edge of the valley, and there he found that his mare had become fidgety and nervous, which was totally unlike his easy-to-manage, old-faithful hunting companion.

When they started up the road out of the valley, Sam sensed that something was following them. Almost instantly his horse started pitching and bucking, which she had never done before. He had to hold onto the saddle-horn to keep from being thrown. Suddenly, without warning, the mare took off at a full gallop. She ran as if she were on a flat racetrack, not a steep, rugged mountain road. As Sam held on for dear life, there was no doubt in his mind that he was being chased by something. He could almost feel a hot breath on the back of his neck — then he heard the blood-curdling screams coming from the valley below.

About halfway up the road the feeling of being chased and the screams from the valley came to an end. Within seconds Sam's horse slowed down to a trot. Until then Sam hadn't noticed that the deer, which he had laid across his lap, was gone. Apparently it had been tossed off when the horse started bucking. Even though that deer was to have been meat for his family, he wasn't about to go back down the road to find it.

Sam, even to this day, is totally confused as to what he had experienced. Maybe he had been chased by a hungry cougar that had picked up the scent of the deer meat — or just maybe the tale Sam heard as a young child is true. His grandfather used to tell him about a valley of death — a small valley tucked away deep in the heart of the Devil's Backbone, where Spanish soldiers were massacred by Apache warriors. The tale has it that occasionally the screams of the massacre can still be heard.

Many years have passed since that cold January night, and Sam has gone hunting when necessary — but, as far as I know, he has never returned to Haunted Valley.

Searching the Backbone

The Devil's Backbone is only an hour's drive from either San Antonio or Austin, so if you are traveling in the vicinity you might want to venture onto Highway 32. Should you decide to pull into the roadside park to enjoy the spectacular views, don't be alarmed if you happen to see Sara and Frank searching the hillsides.

Sara, estimated to be in her mid-thirties, stands about 5'3" tall, with long, blonde hair and a complexion as fair as milk and honey. She has sparkling blue eyes, but there is a certain sadness dominating her sweet facial expressions.

Little Frank has all the energy of a nine or ten-year-old, even though he is somewhat small for his age. Just as Sara, he has blonde hair and deep blue eyes, but again, there is the sadness that even his youthful smile cannot hide.

It was during the late summer of the mid-1980s when Sara and Frank were first seen by Joel. The new foreman had just signed on with the Chaparral Ranch, which is encompassed in the folds of the Devil's Backbone.

Joel, an easy-going, ex-rodeo cowboy, had worked on ranches all of his life so, then at the age of forty-plus years, he was a real asset to the Chaparral. He is a well-built man standing just over 6' tall, and his steel-gray eyes, salt-and-pepper hair, and full beard add to his handsomely rugged look. He always wears blue jeans, long-sleeved shirts, and a leather vest. He wouldn't be caught dead in any footwear other than his high-top cowboy boots, and he usually sports a somewhat weather-beaten cowboy hat. He could easily be mistaken for a character out of the 1800s.

On the afternoon of Joel's first encounter he had been on horseback since daybreak and had traveled many miles checking for gaps in an old fenceline. He still had quite a distance to ride before returning to the ranch headquarters, so he dismounted his steed to seek the shade of a sprawling oak tree. He was guzzling a hefty swig of water from his canteen when out of the corner of his eye he caught a glimpse of a young woman and small boy walking across a meadow some two-hundred yards away. By the time he scrambled to his feet they were nowhere to be seen, but he did spot an old wagon trail at the edge of the meadow. Joel simply assumed the woman and boy were some neighbors out for an afternoon walk.

It was dark when Joel rode into the corral, and after tending to his horse, all he wanted to do was enjoy a good meal and get some sleep.

By the time he served his plate the other ranch hands had already headed to the bunkhouse. The cook was busy cleaning up the kitchen, but as usual she took time to ask Joel how his day had gone. During their brief conversation Joel mentioned seeing some neighbors, and the cook, trying to figure out who they might be, asked where he had seen them. When he described the small meadow and old wagon trail she became perplexed. The cook was positive there wasn't anyone living within walking distance of the remote area he had described.

As Joel drifted off to sleep that night he couldn't stop thinking about the young woman and little boy, and wondering where they had come from.

The next day began a hectic week for everyone on the Chaparral, and Joel was so extremely busy he had completely forgotten about the lady and boy. Then his second encounter took place in a secluded valley nestled between steep canyon walls.

A gentle west wind blew across the Backbone as dawn broke that Sunday, and Joel again mounted-up at daybreak to begin searching for a stray heifer and her newborn calf.

With the hot Texas sun still hidden below the ridge, the early morning hours were pleasantly cool and crisp, but by noon the temperature had climbed into the low nineties. Joel reined his pony at the edge of a spring-fed pond and dismounted to get a drink of the refreshing, cold water.

Within a few minutes a rustling in the brush drew his attention, and seconds later the stray cattle moseyed out to a small clearing only fifty feet away.

Suddenly an unexplained chill came upon Joel, and then the young woman and little boy were standing within petting distance of the cattle, which seemed unaware of the pair's presence.

Joel was spellbound, and all he could do was stare at his two visitors. Judging from their clothing, he was positive they weren't from this day and time, and surely they had just stepped out of the 1800s. The woman was wearing a full-length, long-sleeved, blue gingham dress trimmed with a white collar and cuffs, and the little boy's garb has often been described by Mark Twain. He was dressed in a long-sleeved white shirt, light-blue knickers held up by suspenders, and a pair of brown, ankle-high, lace-up shoes.

When Joel realized they were spirits from the past his reaction was quite different from what you might expect. Instead of being scared or frightened, he felt he needed to offer them help. Perhaps it was the sadness on their faces that caused that reaction.

Even though the words weren't spoken aloud, in Joel's mind he did hear the woman say, "Thank you sir, but you are not of our time." Then she took the boy's hand, and as they vanished Joel heard her say, "Come son, he is not your father."

It has now been over ten years since that Sunday, and several people have encountered the woman, whom we now call Sara, and her son, whom we now call Frank. We can only surmise that the husband and father they are searching for must have met his fate here on the Devil's Backbone. We can only hope that someday they will be reunited.

Joe Angel's Visitors

Sara and Frank (of "Searching the Backbone") left for a visit but now have returned.

It was a cold, wet day towards the end of hunting season when we met Joe Angel, a rather busy young boy who was with his step-father, Alfred "Junior" Kuhlman, a hunting guide on our ranch.

For several months, Joe would visit the ranch whenever Junior would allow him to come. At first, this quiet, little brown-eyed, dark-haired boy seemed to be no more than busy, doing what all little boys like to do when given a chance to visit a ranch or get out with Mother Nature. Joe would throw sticks for the ranch dogs to chase, build rock forts, and pretend that he was truly one of the cowboys from the past. Many times, he walked with his play-gun through the safer areas of the ranch and continued his imaginative pastime.

Joe was a very bright boy of Mexican heritage, and many a time I had thought to myself that his love for the land, coupled with his family's background, might have had something to do with the coming events.

The first time I noticed Joe doing something a little unusual was late one afternoon as he played with

40

our cow-dog, Tippy, a sweet dog that loves children and always protects them from any danger. Joe threw a stick to Tippy, and the stick landed between two large elm trees. These trees are the location of several sightings of the supernatural from the not-so-distant past.

As both Tippy and Joe ran toward the trees, they both came to an abrupt stop. Then they walked up to within inches of the trees. Tippy was looking up and wagging her tail. Joe stood for a moment, and then seemed to be talking to himself.

Within minutes Junior called for Joe to return to the truck. He was in a hurry, and it was getting late. So with little more said, they were gone.

Several months passed, and I had almost forgotten Joe's particular experience. And, with hunting season now well behind us, Junior had very little reason to come to the ranch. Yet, as a friend, he would drop in to visit from time to time.

It was a late afternoon in April that I noticed Junior's truck pulling up outside the ranch house. At first, I thought nothing of his arrival. As I watched him approach the house, I could tell that he definitely had something on his mind. As he reached the back porch, I stepped out to meet him.

Junior asked if I had some time; of course I did. He walked across the yard and squatted down in a kneeling position under a large shade tree. Then he unconsciously pulled his knife from its scabbard and began to whittle on a small piece of oak.

I had taken a seat on a small boulder nearby. Junior then looked up at me and began to speak. "Bert, I know you believe in these ghost things, but I have been very skeptical about this tale. However, I want to pass it along, and maybe you can help me. Joe's mother and I are terribly confused."

I silently nodded in a reassuring manner, for I knew another encounter was about to be told.

Joe had started having strange dreams. He would sit up in his bed and begin to laugh and make gestures, as though he was playing with someone or something. After his mother would awaken him, Joe seemed a little irritated, and would then fall back on his bed and go back to sleep. This happened for several nights. Yet, when Joe was questioned about this event, he would say very little. At first he seemed to shrug it off.

But after six or seven nights of these strange dreams, he decided to talk to his mother and Junior. He had been playing with a young, blonde-headed boy named Frank. They had been playing on the Chaparral ranch.

Joe then described a lady, the young boy's mother. Her name was Sara. She was nice, but she would correct the young boys if it looked as though they were about to get into trouble or possibly have an accident.

Joe then began to describe areas on the ranch that did exist. Yet, due to the potential danger surrounding these areas, young Joe had not been allowed to visit these spots. But his descriptions were completely accurate, even down to the smallest detail.

Junior and I discussed the entire affair, and I suggested that he or Joe's mother should try sending Sara and Frank home.

What I felt they should do was the following: wait until Joe fell asleep, and as soon as he started laughing, instruct Frank and Sara to return to the ranch.

Joe's mother did just as suggested. And to my knowledge, Joe now sleeps through the night without interruption. And for reasons known to us here on the ranch, we are sure Sara and Frank have returned.

The Entrance Gate

What's in a gate? If you live in rural America gates of all types are certainly no stranger to you because, as most of us, you have opened your share. For those urban Americans, I am sure you have noticed them in your out-of-town travels as you have crossed and crisscrossed many highways of the nation.

These entrances can appear extremely auspicious, looming toward the heavens above, generally exposing an individual's false ego for all to see.

Yet, others may never be seen, as they were constructed to serve a true purpose — to keep something in, or something out.

Many things can be said of entrance gates. But that is not my reason for mentioning them. I have a very unusual gate to describe, and the events surrounding its being.

This entrance gate cannot be seen from the highway. It is tucked away deep within the Central Texas hills in the inner regions of the old Devil's Backbone. An individual traveling this winding, climbing, curving highway must have good directions to find this ranch entrance.

You must turn south and continue down an old

dirt road to reach this particular spot. The gate is not unusual. It is similar to most across this vast country, and the old ranch indentification sign is located on the fence next to the gate. It is certainly not ego-oriented. But the past events will be worth noting.

Let me also mention that the old dirt road running past this entrance was once a major cattle trail which led to the city of San Antonio. And during the past century it was a very active crossing through this sacred Indian country.

It was quite some years ago when I started gathering these unusual happenings which in some manner seem to revolve around this non-descript gate.

A young man and his fiancée were visiting family within the confines of this ranch. It was quite late in the evening when the couple decided to return to their home in San Marcos, Texas, which was just a thirty-minute drive from the ranch. The night was exceptionly still and cold, with a milky-white, full moon above. As they approached the gate they couldn't help but notice the ghostly shadows being cast from the large trees which lined the road to the gate.

The young man relatched the gate, slipped behind the wheel of his vehicle — and both he and his bride-to-be were suddenly struck speechless. For there in front of them was the image of an Indian warrior sitting atop a large white horse surrounded by a smoky, ominous haze.

Within seconds the young man sped out into the middle of the state highway. The couple looked at each other for some time before they discussed what they had seen. An Indian from the past? A ghost? They certainly believe so.

Many other occurrences have happened around the gate, and even *to* the gate. One summer while cowboys moved a herd of longhorn cows out of this same gate, and loaded them by truck to ship to another ranch, this gate seemed to continue to re-lock its chain and master lock . . . not just once, but several times during the cattle drive. This really weighed on the cowboys' patience.

The cowboys laughed about it later, but with the hot dust blowing up and a mad herd of longhorns, very little humor was seen at the time this occurred.

A young lady had business at the ranch for a period of several months, so she had to come and go on a regular basis. At first she claimed that she would feel quite apprehensive when she had to open or close the gate. This mild sensation seemed to escalate into a true fear. It became so bad that she insisted her husband come with her on her final journeys to this gate so, that he would handle the chain. It was later learned that the young lady was blessed with a psychic ability, and if she still has business on this ranch, I am sure someone is assisting her with the gate.

This past summer a local businessman stopped by that ranch to say hello, but more than a casual visit developed. It was near dusk when the man came through the gate. A gentle, cooling breeze was now whipping through the trees surrounding the gate. After latching the gate and returning to his car, he couldn't help but notice an Indian astride a large black and white horse. The man yelled and waved to this motionless individual, but the rider did not respond.

Then that visitor took a closer look at the man as he passed him on his continued short drive to the main house. This Indian was definitely dressed as one from the 1800s — an open leather vest, a flat-brimmed black hat, and a large, old, buffalo rifle held in his crossed arms.

Within minutes both the businessman and the rancher returned to the spot where the Indian had been seen. Yet, there were no signs that a rider had been at the location . . . not even a hoofprint could be found.

In further discussion, the rancher informed the businessman that no one of that description was now, or ever had been, employed by the rancher. Was that man a poacher? Had he gotten lost? Or was he possibly a spirit from the past? These questions will probably never be answered.

The gate still stands, and I am sure that some other unsuspecting person will encounter other experiences there in the future.

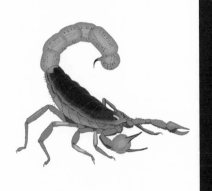

Burning Scorpion

It was late one afternoon on a Saturday when several of our local friends dropped by the ranch. They were on their way to the Devil's Backbone Tavern, and invited us to come along.

Several hours passed. The hot summer day had slipped into a cool, pleasant evening with a most refreshing, light breeze. The Tavern was full of old friends, some of which we had not seen for quite a while. So, for my wife C. D. and I, it had truly turned into a superb evening.

During the evening I noticed a fellow sitting at the opposite end of the room from where our group was seated. It became apparent to me that this man had been studying us for quite some time. He looked to be a rather small, well-built man in his late thirties or early forties. He had coal-black hair with dark, piercing eyes, rather high cheekbones, and a dark-to-reddish complexion.

In my continued observation of the man, several things became more apparent to me. He had not been drinking to any extreme and had said very little to any of the other patrons. Yet, he continued to watch our table.

By late evening it was time to go. As C. D. and I were getting in our truck I heard someone call out our names. I turned around and there he stood. The man quickly introduced himself and very politely asked if he could come by the ranch on the following day. He said he had come some distance to meet us, and needed to talk to us about a matter of some importance. I told the man that our gate would be unlocked by a certain time of the following day, and we would be glad to speak with him if he so desired.

By early afternoon of the following day this stranger had still not arrived, so I began to dismiss the thought of him or his urgent need to visit with us. I was just about to go down to lock the gate when he appeared on foot, walking toward the front porch.

He was dressed in blue jeans with a rawhide vest covering his bare chest. As he came nearer to me, I then noticed his moccasin-styled leather boots. He had some sort of rawhide sash or belt loosely tied around his waist, and a true Indian headband was snugly tied around his forehead, which allowed his ink-black hair to drape down the back of his neck. I could not help but feel that he did truly have some definite purpose at the Devil's Backbone.

I called C. D. when I noticed the man coming up the trail to our home. And when he reached the porch, both C. D. and I were there to greet him. He smiled at both of us, and in an Indian fashion, he shook our hands. It was then that he began to speak.

"I did not give you my true name last night. I could have been Pete or Joe or Charlie or any other white man's name when I introduced myself. It would have made no difference, for in my life I really have but one name, and I carry it on my body as all members of my society do. I am Burning Scorpion, as you can see."

He opened his loosely hanging vest, and there upon his upper abdomen was the cutting and carving of a scorpion, with its tail up and ready to sting anyone or anything in its path. This was not a tattoo as we know them. This was a deep scar which had healed over many years.

I asked him what we could do for him and why he had decided to come to the Devil's Backbone. He answered, "Might we take a seat, and I will try to explain my visit." C. D. had prepared a pitcher of iced tea and had passed each of us a glass, serving the young Indian first.

"Thank you. As I mentioned, I have come a great distance. I am a Mescalero Apache, and my people are located on a large reservation in Arizona. I am from a very small group of full-blooded Mescaleros. We form a society within our large Indian Nation. We still hold on to many of our old customs and old ways. Within our group we have several descendants of the Lipan Apaches and some Kiowas. It is due to one of these old people that I am here, you might say, on his behalf.

"His name is White Eagle. He is quite old now. His ancestors roamed this holy area known as the Devil's Backbone. To his people, and others, your ranch sits atop one of their more spiritual places. He had a vision that the area was almost the same, and that the Anglo had not yet destroyed it, as so many other areas have now been defaced. He wants me to perform a ceremony for him and his people, as he now sees this country soon to fall to the white developer's ways."

With very little further conversation we decided to give Burning Scorpion permission to walk the ranch and enact the sacred ceremony. We only asked him to stop back by the house before he departed so that we would know that he had completed his mission. We both have had a fondness towards the American Indians and felt no harm in this situation.

It was near dark when this strange Apache returned. C. D. invited him to stay for dinner, but he politely refused. He thanked us again, and then informed us that quite a few of the old ancestors were still here. As he started down the walkway, he stopped and then turning, faced us. Again he spoke.

"The Spirits are very protective of both of you; they like the fact that you love this sacred place. And for the most part, you have left the Backbone as it was. Thank you from all of us." With that statement made, the stranger was on his way.

Several days passed. C. D. and I discussed this strange event on numerous occasions, but as so many other strange happenings had occurred along this old Backbone area, we decided not to question why.

Late one evening, just at dark, we had to leave the ranch on an unexpected mission. As we approached the front gate a strong gust of wind blew past us, and the gate flew open. C. D. and I just looked at each other, for we had never seen anything like that happen, before or since. We pulled through the open gate.

I quickly checked the gate for possible damage — there was none. I then checked the old chain latch — it was secure. I walked back to the truck, and as always, I couldn't help but laugh to myself. There I was, trying to rationalize one of hundreds of happenings on the old Backbone.

Soon we were on the highway. As I lit a cigarette, it became apparent to me that C. D. had said little since the gate had so mysteriously opened for our departure. I then questioned her about her silence. With little hesitation she remarked, in a questioning manner, "Didn't you see them — the Indians standing across from the gate?"

I didn't see them, yet I don't doubt they were there. . . .

A Skull from the Past

It was late one spring afternoon when several young men gathered at a predetermined location high atop the Devil's Backbone. They had a specific purpose for the meeting and were quite serious about the task that lay before them.

It seems as though some years prior to this undertaking, one of the men, while hunting deer, had stumbled across what appeared to be an old horizontal mine shaft. This man-made tunnel had several crude, handmade steps leading down into a pit of darkness. It was quite late that particular evening when he made the discovery, and darkness would soon be upon him, so he did not have time to investigate that strange place. As luck would have it, it was the last day of his hunting trip, and he would not return for several years.

Nine to ten years passed before he and his comrades met again at the Backbone. Yet, the young man had thought quite a bit about his find. After all, many tales of lost gold mines and buried treasure abound in this region. And just *maybe* he was on to something big.

He had an unusual group of friends: school teachers, cowboys, service men and others, yet he had picked each in accordance with their honesty and stamina. They were soon at their task, with the young man now retracing his steps.

Moving across a high, windy ridge atop this unusual, winding terrain, with little hesitation he went straight to the spot. He knew this was the right place, yet the hole was not there. The large oaks and cedars seemed to be as he had remembered them. The rough, rocky boulders still jutted out way above the canyon and the wet weather creek below. The cactus, high grasses, and general underbrush was all just as he had remembered it.

An hour or so had now passed before the group took a break. He was both embarrassed and confused. Maybe he was just a mountaintop off, so he decided to have the others spread out and cover hilltops and canyon. All the men were in agreement, so spread out they did. However, this was no easy task, due to the heavy foliage and loose, rocky hillside. One wrong step and someone could get in trouble. All the men were in agreement, so spread out they did.

The young man was still convinced that he was right and that he must scour the area from the top of the hill to the lower creekbed. Yet, it had been almost ten years, and darkness had just about covered him when he first discovered the shaft.

Due to the excitement of the treasure hunt, all the men had failed to stay conscious of the constantly changing spring weather. It had gotten quite hot, and off toward the northwest a large band of blue-black clouds had gathered. And, as conditions would have it, that storm would surely pass across them within the hour.

The young man was walking down the middle of the creekbed when he realized that several of his friends were yelling back and forth to each other. He stopped to listen; maybe they had found what he had been so diligently looking for. But that wasn't the case. He could barely make out their rather anxious calls. "Who the hell was that?" "What the hell was that?" "I don't know.Let's get out of here!"

Now, with the young man standing deep within the creekbed, he looked up toward the high ridges. Above him, the black clouds were rolling across the Backbone as if they were a large wall of boiling smoke. He knew he should take cover.

The winds started blowing, bring heavy rain, and marble-size hail was soon to follow. Lightning flashed and thunder roared, echoing through the canyons. He started up the hill, when the wet rock and dirt caused him to fall back, head-over-heels.

Landing in the now-flowing creek, he regained himself and looked into the shallow water. *A skull, my God, a piece of a human skull!* He hadn't noticed it before. He picked it up and carried it with him, climbing back to the top of the mountain. The rain was not letting up. The lightning still danced across the hills.

He started to trot to the place where they had left their trucks. He suddenly remembered the yelling of his friends — what had they seen? And *where* was the old shaft? He then looked at the old skull. What was going on?

Within minutes he was at the trucks, with the others soon to arrive. He sat trying to dry off, but it was useless.

The storm was rapidly passing. It sooned slow to a sprinkle and then cleared. With this calm replacing the sudden storm, he stepped from the security of the truck.

The men were now arriving, wet and exhausted.

They all gathered around the main truck, helping themselves to some refreshments. Little was said at first, and then several of the men couldn't help but feel compelled to speak.

It seems as though they had seen several Indians — yes, Indians — as many as might comprise a small war party. The Indians had been crossing the hillsides, watching the treasure hunters' every move. Then the skull was shown to the others.

Will the young men return to hunt again? I have no idea, but I was told that a professor at a local university did identify the skull as being that of a human who had died of a nasty blow to the head some 150 years ago. Maybe an axe got him, or possibly a tomahawk. Who knows?

I *do* know where the skull now rests.

The Lady at the Fireplace

It was a warm spring afternoon. We were anticipating the arrival of a new-found friend, an ex-Vietnam veteran and paraplegic.

Jerry Horrigan and I had a lot in common, and through our common interests a true friendship had evolved. Jerry was a native-born Texan; he had been raised in the Texas Hill Country. He had chased a hidden treasure and lost gold mine on his family's ranch for many years.

Often he had heard about us and our precious metal venture. Jerry took the initiative to get in touch, and from that first telephone conversation the friendship began. The ex-UT football star had developed into a well-known songwriter, yet his old, burning desire to find a Spanish treasure never escaped him.

On this particular afternoon a true family meeting was about to now take place. Both C. D., my wife, and I were very close to Jerry, and today we were about to meet Jerry's daughter and her fiancé for the first time.

Our visitors arrived about 3:00 P.M., and after some maneuvering we ended up seated in the ranch house office area. Then the formal introductions were made. The young girl was in her early twenties. She was truly beautiful with long, black, braided hair, an olive complexion, and snapping black eyes. There was no doubt that she was a full-blooded Cherokee, and as we later learned, she was very proud of her ancestry. Yet that did not affect her love for Jerry, who had adopted her at a very young age.

Her name was Charlene, yet she had been nick-named Charlie, and it seemed to stick. It was not too long after the conversation began that I knew that this exceptional young lady was extremely intelligent and very intuitive.

We visited for several hours about lost gold mines and treasures. C. D. and I had purposely stayed away from mentioning any of the strange visions and sightings that had been so prevalent on the Chaparral and across the Devil's Backbone.

It was late in the afternoon. Our visit had been quite interesting and extremely enjoyable. Charlie asked to be excused. C. D. showed her the bathroom, and then my wife immediately returned to the ongoing discussion.

Jerry and I were deep in an historical interpretation of the old *Miranda Report*, which some consider the Bible of all Texas treasure and lost gold mine hunters.

Some time seemed to pass before Charlie returned and quietly took her seat. She seemed to be preoccupied with something. From time to time she glanced back down the hallway toward the living room.

Late evening was upon us, and it was time for the veteran and his family to depart.

Several hours passed before a phone call came in, and the story then unfolded. It was Jerry. At first he hemmed and hawed around, and then he got down to brass tacks.

On her return from the bathroom Charlie had seen an old woman sitting in a chair next to the fireplace in the living room. It was only after Charlie tried to strike up a conversation with the woman that she realized that this well-dressed, gray-haired lady was definitely a ghost.

Jerry then told me about certain psychic abilities Charlie possessed. It seems that she discovered her abilities when she was a very young girl. Yet, she had never said much about it to anyone outside of her immediate family.

It turned out that Charlie felt that the old lady had "traveled" back to their home with them, and that she would see the woman again.

In about a week I received a letter from Jerry. They were in the process of moving out of state, but he wanted me to know that Charlie had seen the lady again.

It was late one night, just before midnight, when Charlie was awakened with someone tugging on her bedcovers. It was the old lady. She wanted Charlie's help in finding a missing file — papers concerning her past and the history of the Devil's Backbone. She had misplaced the papers just before her demise, and felt that these historical documents might help us in our quest to find what has been long-hidden on the Backbone.

Charlie never saw the woman again, yet we are sure she is still around.

The Old Yellow Lantern

The first time this mysterious glow was noticed around the old ranch house it didn't seem to cause much discussion, or arouse much interest . It was early one cold December morning just before daybreak.

My wife had arisen quite early. She had quite a bit of paper work to catch up on, and for her, early morning hours are always the best. She was sitting at the desk, which faces a large, double floor-to-ceiling window, and as one sits at the desk one can't help but notice any movement that might take place outside these windows.

C. D. had just refilled her coffee cup from the pot nearby, and as she looked up to take a sip of thick, steeping-hot brew, she noticed an eerie light which was moving from left to right and casting a small, yellow glow. It was not a type of light that she was familiar with. It certainly did not have the color or brightness of a flashlight, or even a gas lantern. The color was too yellow, and the haze around this light seemed to give off some sort of unfamiliar gas or glow. The light appeared to move up and down, as if it were being carried. It was not visible for long, yet it was long

59

enough to know that it was not a figment of her imagination, or due to eye strain from the close paper work she was doing.

As the day unfolded, we were extremely busy running errands. So it was late in the evening before C. D. described what she had seen earlier that morning. Both Joel and I listened as the event was described. There have been so many unexplained happenings around the Devil's Backbone, and Joel, our foreman, had certainly had his share of strange, inexplicable occurrences as he went about his daily activities.

Several months passed before the light was seen again. It was now early spring. And quite late one evening, as I was standing, gazing into the darkness out of the large office windows, I saw the unexplained light. It was definitely moving across the top ridge, and as best I could figure, it was near an old mineshaft from which we had previously taken samples. Was this a transient, a poacher? Or maybe a curious individual wondering if we had found anything of real value in our exploration?

The following day both C. D. and I covered the hillside looking for anything that might give us a clue to the strange light. By now I was convinced that we had seen some sort of antique, oil lantern, one very similar to that of my grandmother's, which had been passed down through our family for generations — one *definitely* not from this time period.

By late afternoon we had covered every possible trail that the light could have traveled. It was then that C. D. decided to take a quick look at the old mineshaft. I had drifted off in another direction when, all at once C. D. called for me to come look. As I approached the shaft, I could tell that C. D. was standing motionless, staring down into the darkness. As I looked down into the deep slice in the ground, I saw a lantern, an old rusty lantern! With little said, I retrieved this old relic from the shaft. We had worked in that shaft for months, and this strange contraption had not previously been there.

That night we examined the old oil lantern, and two things became very apparent: (1) it was definitely from the mid-1800s; and (2) it was so rusty it could not have worked anytime within this century.

Oh, in closing, I must add that the strange light has not been seen since.

The Mineshaft Mystery

It was a cold, gray December day, with no more than an hour left before dark would engulf this small, Devil's Backbone valley. The loud crack of a high-powered rifle being fired echoed throughout the hills.

George had been sitting in a large, burr oak tree some thirty feet or more above this calm valley, taking deadly aim at a huge, reddish-brown boar. George was an excellent shot, so the hog went down with only one bullet.

George tied his rifle to a rope and safely lowered it to the ground. Then he cautiously started his descent out of the tree. It was then he saw something that he knew he shouldn't be seeing. Peering through the branches of this majestic tree, he saw a cave, or more like an opening similar to an old mineshaft. It was across the valley and up the side of a high hill.

George rubbed his eyes to clear the half-frozen mist which had begun to fall. He knew the country well. He had climbed, crawled, walked, and ridden horseback across this country many times in the past. He knew that there were no mineshafts in that area.

As darkness approached, he saw a figure of a man, but then it seemed to disappear into the cedar breaks.

George yelled out to the man, but there was no response. A still quiet had again fallen across the valley.

George's main interest reverted back to the reality of both the hour of the evening and pulling this large boar back to the main ranch house, which was over a mile away. He entered the valley earlier that afternoon on horseback, and now after fastening the rope from the hog to his saddlehorn, he began his trek out of the valley.

Within a couple of days George visited the rancher, who at first was as sure as George that no cave or mineshaft existed along that high ridge. Yet, the old cowman knew George as an honest cowboy with a good head on his shoulders. They must check it out together, they decided, so with little else said, both men made plans to visit the high-ridged valley.

For the next few days, as George went about his daily activities, he couldn't help but think about the mysterious mineshaft.

Due to a previous experience the rancher witnessed, he had no doubt that he could lead George to the place the mineshaft was seen. Several years earlier a young psychic lady had been on the ranch. She, the rancher, and several others had gone to the same valley George had hunted the day he saw the mineshaft. While the psychic was there, she led the way out of the valley and up a hill to a spot where she claimed she could see an ancient mineshaft. All anyone else in the group could see was the grayed, weathered rock ledge.

The rancher and George climbed into the pickup truck to search for the cave, or mineshaft. Until then, the rancher hadn't told George about the psychic or her vision. George didn't understand why the rancher had asked, but he agreed to let the rancher lead the way up the hillside. When they stopped, George became a little unnerved. They were at the spot where he had seen the mineshaft — but where was it? And how did the rancher know that was the spot?

When the rancher told George about the psychic he did feel a little better. But to this day George can't understand why he was able to see the mineshaft that wasn't there. And what about the man George saw that day while hunting? Could he be another spirit that roams the Devil's Backbone?

Old Barn Spirit

It never ceases to amaze me, the time one takes before relating a story of an event that happened while on the Devil's Backbone. And this tale is certainly no exception.

It was a warm spring day when Bill, one of our cowboy friends. stopped by. It had *only* taken him approximately twelve years to tell me of this ghostly happening.

He and another young fellow, Mike, worked on this Hill Country ranch during the summer of 1982. They were laborers during a major re-fencing project which was under way, and part of their compensation included living in the barn on the ranch.

For the first month or so nothing out of the ordinary happened to these new ranch residents, just scorching hot days and back-breaking work from early in the morning 'till the dusky late evening started to cool this hellish countryside.

The men had developed their own routine as each day's work would come to an end. They first took a dip in the cold, spring-fed, earthen cattle tank, then hopped in the ranch pickup truck, put it in 4-wheel drive, and climbed out of the deep, lush valley, arriving at the barn. Then, with little said, they opened the barn doors, lit the lanterns, and started the evening meal.

It was a welcome relief to feel the cool, gentle breeze moving through the branches of the large oak trees surrounding this rustic, old barn. Both men would sit on their makeshift stools, consuming their meal and visiting about the day's activities.

It was usually about then that the old rancher would pass by to visit a minute and continue on his way home. This had also become a part of their evening routine. And, as I previously mentioned, nothing unusual had happened, at least not until the following event occurred.

It was late one night after both young men had turned in, when Bill awoke to the sound of a hammer hitting something. He lay there in his army-style cot, attempting to fully wake up. Then he reached for his watch and flashlight — it was three o'clock in the morning! Now fully awake, he glanced toward his partner's bunk. Mike was fast asleep.

After slipping on his jeans and boots, Bill quickly moved toward the open door. The sound now became more pronounced to him. It was the sound of a hammer, and possibly a chisel, striking rock. He stood silently, getting his bearings on the direction of this late night sound. It was coming from a rocky canyon some three or four hundred yards away, directly in front of the old barn.

Soon the hammering ceased. Bill stood for some time, continuing to listen, but it had definitely stopped.

After returning to his cot, Bill glanced again at his

pocket watch. It was now a quarter of four. He developed an uneasy feeling as he drifted off to sleep.

Bill only mentioned this event in passing to Mike, but stayed alert for several nights before the following situation took place.

It a Friday,payday, so both men broke their usual routine. They returned late, around midnight, after taking in a country dance at one of the local bars. And in their half-inebriated state it didn't take too long to fall into bed and a deep sleep.

Several hours had passed when Bill woke with a start. He had an uneasy feeling as he looked through the large, open barn doors. The summer's full moon cast long shadows across the open area. In the moon's glow Bill saw a man, definitely an older man, who was moving from left to right across the barn entrance.

Bill grabbed his shotgun which lay across his cot, and then he bolted unright in his bed. Could this be the old rancher? Certainly not at this late hour. The old man was dressed in clothing from the past and seemed to be carrying some sort of pick, or maybe an axe. Bill was not sure.

Now fully awake, he yelled out to the man. "Stop! Who are you?" The man turned and looked straight at the cowboy, as if the old fellow was trying to communicate with this worker — but then suddenly he just disappeared.

By now Mike was well awake. He addressed his partner. But with little said, both men scurried out the door. There was no one there . . . not a living soul.

It was hard to keep their minds on their work as the days passed, one melting into another. Both men seemed to grow more uneasy. They slept with loaded shotguns beside their bunks, safeties off.

Little things seemed to be moved . . . tools now

seemed to disappear and then reappear. Nothing was stolen or taken, yet it was absolutely apparent that someone, or something wanted its presence known.

It was a good three weeks since they saw the old man. On this particular evening the large Plexiglas doors to the barn had to be closed due to the threat of an oncoming thunderstorm. It didn't take too long for an onslaught of storms to begin. Thunder, lightning, and large hailstones pelted the tin roof. It was certainly a night to be inside.

Both men had eaten supper early, and with nothing left to do during these hellish storms, they decided to play some poker. They faced the barn doors as they played, and as the lightning danced about, they could see out through the doors.

Lightning ripped the skies, and in the sudden, illuminating flash Mike and Bill saw the old man standing, peering in at them. The hailstones were so large they smashed loudy against the tin roof. They practically had to scream to be heard above the din. They were both in shock as they sat dumbfounded, staring at the old man. The hail seemed to be going right *through* him. *No one* could have made it through such a storm, not standing in its midst without cover.

Soon Mike moved quickly to the door. Now bracing himself, Mike opened the large entrance door and yelled to the old gentleman to come in. Yet no one did . . . no one came forward . . . no one was there. . . .

The two cowboys finished out the week, and with little said, they left and never returned, not until Bill told me this Devil's Backbone story. He just wanted someone to know of his experience. And as Bill stood to leave, facing the same old barn, it was apparent to me that a chill shot up his spine.

One Named Jesse

One of our friends in the Central Texas area is a well-known horse trainer and a true cowgirl in every sense of the word.

She was raised on a rough-country ranch, and like most children at that time, she worked along with her family to make ends meet. Yet, she enjoyed the ranch work and ranch life as much as any male could have hoped to like this hard, strenuous, sunup-to-sundown type of existence. She was at home in the rough-country.

As our friend was now in her mid-forties, she had proven herself over and over again as one fine, all-around horse trainer.

It was a cold, gray, misty, late afternoon, and I was preparing the house for another cold night that was soon to be upon us. And it looked to be a cold evening, indeed.

I had just brought in the final supply of firewood, which should see us through the night, when I noticed the cowgirl walking up the rock walk to the ranch house office door. She was a rather small woman, yet quite muscular. She had a pretty, smiling face, even though she had that weathered skin, so common for

69

anyone who had been outdoors in the predominately hot, arid climate. Without thinking, I motioned for her to come on in.

By the time she was in, my wife C. D. immediately offered her a cup of hot coffee. And needless to say, it was not refused. The cowgirl made her visit quite short. She had brought two young, unbroken fillies with her, and she wanted to use our corral for a week or so.

This was certainly no problem, so within a few minutes she unloaded the stock and was on her way.

By early afternoon of the following day I returned to the ranch after making a short trip into San Marcos. When I pulled in at the main gate, I could see the cowgirl sitting on a log next to the corral. She seemed to be gazing off in space. It was apparent to me that she was not aware of my arrival.

The weather was cold and damp with a completely overcast sky. A strange feeling came over me after I had closed the gate and started toward her. I knew something must have happened to this well-adjusted, country girl for she was definitely lost in thought.

I continued on past the corral; she nodded and smiled as I went by. I had decided not to stop and question her. After all, this lady was a rancher, and as most country people, they really don't like to be put through the third degree. And if you wait, you will usually hear the whole story just as it happened.

I busied myself around the house. I had a deadline to meet on another story for our local newspaper, and it needed to be finished that particular afternoon.

Several hours passed before the cowgirl entered the house. She quietly went to the pitcher and poured us a large, hot cup of coffee. She then quietly nodded to C. D. that she should join both of us in the office.

As the ladies took a seat, I knew that C. D. and I were about to travel down a path that had become all too familiar to us. Believe me, you can tell when someone has been visited by a spirit from the past.

Several minutes passed before the cowgirl began to talk. She began with a rather nervous laugh. "Hey, you'all, I am not crazy. Let's get that understood. And if we were not such good friends, I would not be sitting here relaying this thing to you both.

"Both you two had left early. The ranch was void of people, with the exception of me, of course. After working with the ponies for several hours, I decided to take a break.

"I had an uneasy feeling for most of the morning, you know, as if I was being watched. Yet I shrugged this feeling aside. The day had become gloomier. A light fog had drifted in around the corral. I poured a cup of coffee and lit a smoke.

"I sat down on the oak log next to the stalls within the corral, and for the moment, I had thrown off this feeling of being watched. It was then that this tapping on my left shoulder happened. Believe me, it was not my imagination. I quickly turned, full well expecting to see one of you, yet I knew that neither one of you had returned — you guessed it . . . no one was there.

"I got up. I shook all over as if a chill went right through me. I then threw down the cigarette. I walked around the entire corral. I was really shook, 'cause I knew no living human being was within miles of me.

"By now, some thirty minutes or so had passed. I still didn't believe my feelings about that shoulder tapping. Of course by now I had come up with quite a few logical explanations."

Now the lady laughed again before continuing. "It

was then I . . . well . . . I saw him, standing across the corral from me. He was at the edge of the woods, which drops into the large creekbed. Fog seemed to surround him. A man in his late fifties, maybe, dressed as a cowhand, but not like we dress in this day and time — maybe 1840s or 1850s, I don't know, but a long time ago.

"Now as crazy as this sounds, as far away as he was, and the weather like it was, I could see his blue, steel, piercing eyes. It was as if he could look right through me. He then smiled, a nice glowing smile. I didn't feel threatened. I felt all warm inside.

"I then yelled out to the guy. He didn't answer, at least not out loud, but I can tell you his name is Jesse.

"Then it happened. He went up in a mist, or faded into the fog, or just disintegrated in front of my eyes.

"Now the fact is, I feel I will see him again some day. I can't tell you why I have that feeling, but I do."

Nightfall was now upon us. The winds had picked up. A frozen mist was splashing against the office windows. Somehow, I knew the cowgirl was right. Jesse would be back.

Hunter's Story

Deer season was upon us again, and, as so many past seasons, we had taken our time in selecting the right group of hunters to lease part of our Devil's Backbone ranch for the season. You have to be careful in leasing a ranch. You definitely want the right kind of hunters. Safety is all-important, because the rifles used in hunting large game could also be used in a combat situation.

This particular season was one of those selective years, and by the time we made our choice, we were happy with this new group of hunters. This group were all employees of a rather nice-sized oil company. They had hunted as a group in the past, and with the exception of an occasional beer from time to time, they were very safety-minded, and limited the beer drinking to the evening hours after the day's hunt was over.

The group numbered ten people, with only seven members of the group hunting at any given time. This, again, was one of the several ranch safety rules which were to be adhered to at all times. Even though the group was employed by one company, there were

73

two husband and wife hunting combinations, with the other three being one woman and two more men.

The opening weekend of deer season is always a full hunt. In other words, every hunter shows up, especially since the weather is generally okay — not too hot, not too cold.

As the season progresses, the hunting parties seem to diminish in number, and by early December we are usually down to true knowledgeable hunters who border on being professionals. That season was no exception. By mid-December we saw the same four hunters every weekend. The two couples now had acclimated themselves to the ranch and were very aware of where they were and what they were doing.

That particular weekend started as any other, with only one difference. The entire Hill Country was preparing for a true, blue norther, which was to blow in at any time.

It was near dark when both couples arrived at camp. Within a short period of time they had the camp-house ready for business. The fire in the wood cook-stove was now crackling and popping, the kerosene lanterns lit and burning. Their portable radio was playing loudly as all four were truly enjoying themselves. Cathy and Robert had arrived first, with Pete and Sally not far behind.

By dark the four had everything under control. The camp meal of steak, french fries and cole slaw was served. Anticipation was running high. The big deer would certainly move when this artic blast came in. And if it came in wet with snow and ice, all four hunters might land a large Boone and Crockett trophy.

It was during the night that the cold front blew in. The icy winds shifted to the north, and by the early morning hours a blowing snow started to cover the ground.

Pete had been up several times during the night, adding wood to the fire and checking the cabin doors and windows, yet the other three had slept through the wintry arrival. It was just before daybreak, and Pete prepared a breakfast fit for a king, so with very little encouragement needed, the small group devoured every last morsel.

It was time for them to load up and head out to their stands. A last minute check of several items was made by each hunter. Rifles, cartridges, small knapsack with necessities for such a cold, wintry day, and a small thermos of coffee was included. Both Pete and Robert had started their trucks some thirty minutes prior to departure to be sure that the trucks would be ready when they were.

With little said, all four were on their way to their stand. They decided to spend the entire day hunting and not return until after dark. All four were familiar with good hunting techniques, so for them this gray, cold, snowy day was perfect.

Both trucks were parked in open areas where each of the four hunters could easily return if a problem were to arise. Just after daybreak all four had made their way to their deer stands. These deer stands were definitely unique in their way; they had been built some fifteen to eighteen years prior to this particular deer season, but with annual maintenance they had been kept in good order. It is not to say that they had all the comforts of home in the stands, but they had been built to protect a hunter from the wintry elements.

The day went by quite swiftly, and as Pete sat in his high mountain ridge stand, he knew that if he was going to kill a deer, he must take one soon, because dark would come swiftly on a gray, cold day such as that one.

He had heard several shots during the day, and with his knowledge of directions he felt that at least two of the other three had gotten their bucks. Pete had watched several small herds come and go, and at one time he had been tempted to go ahead and take a small-framed, 8-point buck — but it was not really what he had been hunting for. The series of trails which crossed this high ridge stand had to be closely watched, because not all of the deer would walk straight out to the corn feeder. The older animals would tend to stay back in the heavy, brushy cover.

The snow was falling in heavier amounts, yet the winds had died out. A true quiet covered the entire countryside. Pete stared out the small, open window of this rather old deer stand. He placed his full vision and full concentration on the feeder. He knew that if anything was to be harvested today it would have to happen within just a few minutes, or his cold, snowy hunt would be in vain.

Just then he heard a noise he couldn't identify — a snorting, high-pitched sound. A chill went up Pete's neck. He really didn't know what he had heard. Within seconds he witnessed a sight that sent him into true shock. Under the feeder, standing tall, he could see a pair of red eyes, large red eyes — they must have been at least eight inches apart! Smoke seemed to billow from this unidentified creature's large nostrils.

It was dark. Pete slipped the safety forward on his rifle, yet he was not sure of what he was seeing. *What the heck was this thing? Where did it come from?* It must have been six feet tall. Pete rubbed his eyes with his wet, snowy gloves. He began to shake, yet not from the cold. He looked down at the floor of the stand, shaking his head in disbelief. Finally, he looked back up — the red eyes were gone.

Yes, this creature had left just as quickly as it had appeared. Or had it disappeared? What was it? God only knew.

Pete moved quickly toward the safety of his truck. Continually looking behind him toward the stand and feeder, he crossed a rather narrow area maybe six feet wide and twenty feet long, and for a moment he thought this creature was breathing down his neck.

Pete quickly opened the door of the truck. He threw his rifle in the cab, and without hesitation he slammed the door, started the truck, and was off.

He approached Cathy's stand. Pete's senses seemed to be coming back to him, and the feeling of fear left him bit by bit. His headlights caught a glimpse of Cathy as she stood by the road, waiting for Pete and the warmth of the truck.

She waved and pointed — a large buck lay on the ground beside her. Pete pulled up and stopped, and within minutes the buck was loaded in the back of the truck, and the two headed back to the camphouse. Cathy attempted to start a conversation, but Pete just smiled, nodded, and said little.

The hunters broke camp early the next morning and returned to the city.

I didn't see Pete again until early May of the next year. That is when he relayed this story to me.

Mystic Herd

It was only forty short years after the last tribe of Indians were removed from this region of Central Texas that this tale first surfaced.

It seems as though a herd of white deer had been seen by several cowboys as they were on their way back to Wimberley one evening. The men didn't take a shot at the unusual animals because the herd was too far away and darkness would soon engulf the tired horsemen.

The story circulated through the area for several years, but due to the fact that no on else saw these strange animals, almost all the local citizens decided that these fun-loving cowboys must have had a little too much "bug juice" on that particular evening, and their eyes were just playing tricks on them.

Many years passed before the following report circulated through this same area. The exact year and date is not known to this writer, but it was in the late 1940s when this next sighting took place.

It was late, some time just past midnight, when the rancher and his foreman started to make the turn back towards Wimberley on old Ranch Road 12, at an area now known as the "Junction." His old pickup truck headlights scanned the small open pasture as he started the right-hand turn. And there, standing as if frozen, he saw a large, white buck. And in the foreground they counted seven bone-white does. The rancher quickly brought his truck to a stop.

Both men were in awe as they continued to look at these magnificent animals. All of a sudden a cold, chilling breeze blew through the cab of the old pre-WWII truck. And then the deer were gone. Both cowboys were baffled. Where had they gone, and how?

After word passed through the small communities of Wimberley and Blanco, more people were surely on the lookout for these unique animals.

Yet many unanswered questions seemed to take root. How could they have been seen many decades before, and then not again 'till then? After all, there were working ranches throughout the country. Someone would have surely seen these animals grazing the hills! Yet no one, from rancher to hunter, had ever seen them on any of the neighboring ranches.

The white deer have been reportedly seen again since that late-Forties account. Yet this time they were up on the Devil's Backbone, always seen at night, and never during the daylight hours.

And still no *hunter* has mentioned seeing them. Could they be the spirits of the Apache? For the Indians believed that both a white buffalo or a white deer was a good and honorable spirit, always to be worshipped.